THE CHINESE DREAM OF THE GREAT REJUVENATION OF THE CHINESE NATION

XI JINPING

Compiled by
The Party Literature Research Office of the Central Committee
of the Communist Party of China

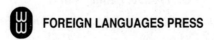 **FOREIGN LANGUAGES PRESS**

First Edition 2014

ISBN 978-7-119-08696-5
© Foreign Languages Press Co. Ltd, Beijing, China, 2014
Published by Foreign Languages Press Co. Ltd
24 Baiwanzhuang Road, Beijing 100037, China
Distributed by China International Book Trading Corporation
35 Chegongzhuang Xilu, Beijing 100044, China
P.O. Box 399, Beijing, China
Printed in the People's Republic of China

Note for Publication

Shortly after the closing of the Eighteenth National Congress of the Communist Party of China (CPC), Xi Jinping, the newly elected General Secretary of the CPC Central Committee, went to the National Museum of China with other Chinese leaders on November 29, 2012, to view the exhibition "The Road of Rejuvenation" about the modern Chinese nation's 100-year struggle. After viewing the exhibition Xi Jinping said that everyone has ideals and aspirations as well as dreams and that achieving the great rejuvenation of the Chinese nation has been the greatest dream of the Chinese people since modern times.

That was the first time a Chinese leader spoke of the Chinese Dream, and it vividly expressed the common ideal and aspiration of the Chinese people. In the speech he gave in March 2013 after he was elected President of China, Xi Jinping discussed the Chinese Dream in greater detail. He noted that realizing the Chinese Dream of the great rejuvenation of the Chinese nation means making the country prosperous and strong, rejuvenating the nation, and making the people happy. Since then he has, on a number of occasions, further addressed many questions concerning the Chinese Dream, such as how to realize it and its relation to the world.

This book, the purpose of which is to help readers come to understand the true nature of the Chinese Dream, consists of 146 expositions from more than 50 documents of Xi Jinping's between

November 15, 2012, and November 2, 2013, including speeches, discussions, letters and instructions. Some of these expositions are published here in English for the first time.

Editor
February 2014

CONTENTS

I

WE ARE REALIZING THE CHINESE DREAM OF THE GREAT REJUVENATION OF THE CHINESE NATION

Our nation is a great nation. Throughout our civilization's more than 5,000 years of development, the Chinese nation made indelible contributions to the progress of human civilization. Since modern times, our nation has gone through untold tribulations and faced its gravest peril. Throughout that time, countless people with lofty ideals rose up in order to achieve the great rejuvenation of the Chinese nation, but each time they failed. After the Communist Party of China (CPC) was founded, it rallied and led the people in making great sacrifices, forging ahead against all odds, and transforming poor and backward old China into an increasingly prosperous and powerful new China, thus opening completely new horizons for the great rejuvenation of the Chinese nation. Our responsibility now is to rally and lead the entire Party and the people of all China's ethnic groups in taking on this task, and continuing to strive to achieve the great rejuvenation of the Chinese nation, so that the Chinese nation can stand firmer and stronger on its own feet among the world's nations and make new and even greater contributions to humankind.

—Excerpt from a speech at a press conference held by members of the Standing Committee of the Political Bureau of the Eighteenth CPC Central Committee, November 15, 2012

Everyone has ideals and ambitions and their own dreams. At present, we are all discussing the Chinese Dream. In my opinion, achieving the great rejuvenation of the Chinese nation has been the greatest dream of the Chinese people since modern times. This dream embodies a long-cherished hope of several generations of Chinese people, reflects the overall interests of the Chinese nation and the Chinese people, and is a shared aspiration of all sons and daughters of the Chinese nation. History informs us that each person's future and destiny are closely linked to those of their country and nation. One can do well only when one's country and nation do well.

...

I firmly believe that the goal of finishing building a moderately prosperous society in all respects can be achieved by 2021 when the CPC celebrates its centenary; the goal of building China into a modern socialist country that is prosperous, strong, democratic, culturally advanced, and harmonious can be achieved by 2049 when the People's Republic of China marks its centenary; and the dream of the great rejuvenation of the Chinese nation will be realized.

—*Excerpts from a speech at the exhibition "The Road of Rejuvenation," November 29, 2012*

Achieving the great rejuvenation of the Chinese nation has been the greatest dream of the Chinese people since modern times. It can be said that this dream is to make our country and our military strong. To achieve the great rejuvenation of the Chinese nation, we must both enrich the country and strengthen the military, and strive to build a strong national defense and powerful military.

—*Excerpt from speeches during an inspection tour of the Guangzhou Military Theater of Operations, December 8 and 10, 2012*

Finishing building a moderately prosperous society in all respects and building China into a modern socialist country that is prosperous, strong, democratic, culturally advanced and harmonious; and realizing the Chinese Dream of the great rejuvenation of the Chinese nation, in other words, making the country prosperous and strong, rejuvenating the nation, and making the people happy, deeply embody the ideals of Chinese people today and reflect our forefathers' glorious tradition of tirelessly striving for progress.

—*Excerpt from a speech at the First Session of the Twelfth National People's Congress (NPC), March 17, 2013*

Realizing the Chinese Dream of the great rejuvenation of the Chinese nation has been the long-cherished dream of the Chinese people since modern times. After the Opium War of 1840, the Chinese nation experienced a century of foreign invasion and civil war and the Chinese people endured extreme misery and pain and suffered an unfortunate fate. The Chinese people champion the Chinese Dream from the bottom of their hearts because it is first and foremost a dream shared by the 1.3 billion Chinese people.

—Answer to a question in a joint interview with reporters from BRICS countries, March 19, 2013

Achieving the great rejuvenation of the Chinese nation has been the greatest dream of the Chinese people since modern times; we call it the Chinese Dream. Its basic idea is to make the country prosperous and strong, rejuvenate the nation, and make the people happy.

—Excerpt from the speech "Follow the Trend of the Times and Promote Peace and Development in the World," at the Moscow State Institute of International Relations, March 23, 2013

The Eighteenth National Party Congress set forth a master blueprint for finishing building a moderately prosperous society in all respects and accelerating socialist modernization and it issued a call for achieving the Two Centenary Goals.[1] We made clear our desire to realize the Chinese Dream of the great rejuvenation of the Chinese nation in accordance with the guiding principles of the congress. At present, everyone is discussing the Chinese Dream and thinking about how it relates to them and what they need to do to achieve it.

…

The Chinese Dream pertains to the past and the present but also the future. The Chinese Dream is the crystallization of the tireless efforts of countless people with lofty ideals, embraces the yearnings of all sons and daughters of the Chinese nation, and beckons a bright future in which our country is prosperous and strong, the nation flourishes and the people live happy lives.

—Excerpts from a speech to outstanding young people from all walks of life, May 4, 2013

The Chinese nation has emerged resilient from trials and tribulations, and it never gave up the pursuit of its beautiful dreams. Realizing the Chinese Dream of the

---

[1] They are to finish building a moderately prosperous society in all respects by the centenary of the CPC (2021) and build China into a modern socialist country that is prosperous, strong, democratic, culturally advanced, and harmonious by the centenary of the People's Republic of China (2049).

great rejuvenation of the Chinese nation has been a long-cherished dream of the Chinese people since modern times.

In this new historical period, the essence of the Chinese Dream is to make our country prosperous and strong, revitalize the nation, and make the people happy. Our objectives are to double the 2010 GDP and per capita income of urban and rural residents and finish building a moderately prosperous society in all respects by 2020. By mid-century, we aim to build China into a modern socialist country that is prosperous, strong, democratic, culturally advanced, and harmonious; and realize the Chinese Dream of the great rejuvenation of the Chinese nation.

—Answer to a question in a joint interview with reporters from Trinidad and Tobago, Costa Rica and Mexico, May 2013

Realizing the Chinese Dream of the great rejuvenation of the Chinese nation is the common aspiration of the people of all China's ethnic groups. To this end, we will continue to give top priority to development; put people first; persist in reform and opening up; comprehensively promote economic, political, cultural, social, and ecological progress; and spur coordinated progress of every aspect of the modernization drive.

—Excerpt from the congratulatory letter to the 2013 Fortune Global Forum in Chengdu, June 5, 2013

At present, the whole Party and the people of all ethnic groups across the country are working vigorously to achieve the objectives set forth at the Eighteenth National Party Congress and forging ahead to realize the Chinese Dream of the great rejuvenation of the Chinese nation. This is the thrust of the Party and country's work, and also the theme of the youth movement in today's China.

—*Remark in a discussion with the new leading body of the Central Committee of the Chinese Communist Youth League, June 20, 2013*

The dream of space travel is an important part of the dream of making the country strong. As China's space program develops rapidly, Chinese people will explore deeper into space.

—*Excerpt from a telephone conversation with Shenzhou 10 astronauts Nie Haisheng, Zhang Xiaoguang, and Wang Yaping while they were orbiting in the space module Tiangong 1, June 24, 2013*

Entering a new era of ecological progress and building a beautiful China are an important part of realizing the Chinese Dream of the great rejuvenation of the Chinese nation. On the basis of the idea of respecting, conforming to and conserving nature, China will carry out the basic state policy of conserving resources and protecting the environment; promote green, circular, and low-carbon development more purposefully; incorporate ecological progress into all aspects and the entire process of economic, political, cultural, and social development; form geographical patterns, industrial structures, modes of production and lifestyles that save resources and protect the environment; and ensure that future generations have a blue sky, green fields, and clean water.

—Excerpt from the congratulatory letter to the 2013 Eco Forum Global Annual Conference in Guiyang, July 18, 2013

Building China into a maritime power is an important component of socialism with Chinese characteristics. The Eighteenth National Party Congress set forth a major plan for making China a strong maritime country. Implementing this plan is of immense and far-reaching significance for promoting sustained, healthy economic development; safeguarding China's sovereignty, security, and development interests; and finishing building a moderately prosperous society in all respects and then achieving the great rejuvenation of the Chinese nation.

—Excerpt from a speech at the Eighth Group Study Session of the Political Bureau of the Eighteenth CPC Central Committee, July 30, 2013

Since the founding of the People's Republic of China over 60 years ago and in particular since adoption of the reform and opening up policy more than 30 years ago, China has blazed a successful path of development and has made remarkable achievements in this regard. China has made strategic arrangements and set clear objectives for its future development, namely, to double its 2010 GDP and per capita income of its urban and rural residents and finish building a moderately prosperous society in all respects by 2020; and by mid-century, to turn China into a modern socialist country that is prosperous, strong, democratic, culturally advanced, and harmonious; and realize the great rejuvenation of the Chinese nation. This is a century-old aspiration of the Chinese nation and its people. It is also a prerequisite for China to make even greater contributions to humankind.

—Excerpt from the speech "Hand in Hand Building a China-ASEAN Community of Shared Destiny," to the Indonesian Parliament, October 3, 2013

Achieving the great rejuvenation of the Chinese nation has been the greatest dream of the Chinese people since modern times. Ever since Dr. Sun Yat-sen first gave voice to the slogan, "Regenerate China," the Chinese nation and the Chinese people have struggled relentlessly and made enormous efforts and sacrifices to attain that goal. Our Party led the people in founding the People's Republic of China following an extremely arduous, protracted struggle more than 60 years ago and in starting to carry out reform and opening up more than 30 years ago. These two great events significantly sped up the historical course of achieving the great rejuvenation of the Chinese nation.

...

The Chinese Dream is a vivid expression, the greatest common divisor, and a view that can be readily accepted by the public. Its central meaning is the great rejuvenation of the Chinese nation, which can be expanded as appropriate, but should never become detached from the theme of the great rejuvenation of the Chinese nation. We must firmly focus on this theme and use it to activate and circulate positive energy.

—Excerpts from a group discussion with the new leading body of the All-China Federation of Trade Unions, October 23, 2013

II

THE CHINESE DREAM
IS IN THE END THE DREAM
OF THE PEOPLE

Our people are a great people. Over the long course of history, the Chinese people, with their toil, courage and wisdom, have created a beautiful homeland in which all ethnic groups live in amity and which has nurtured a splendid culture that is timeless and forever new. Our people love life and yearn for better education, more stable jobs, more satisfactory income, greater social security benefits, better medical and health services, more comfortable living conditions and a more beautiful environment. They want their children to grow up well and have better jobs and more fulfilling lives. Our goal is to satisfy the people's yearning for a better life.

—Excerpt from a speech at a press conference held by the members of the Standing Committee of the Political Bureau of the Eighteenth CPC Central Committee, November 15, 2012

Improving people's lives through economic development is the fundamental goal of all the Party and country's work. If our Party is to strengthen its position as the ruling party and fulfill its mission when in power, it must take fulfilling, safeguarding, and developing the fundamental interests of the overwhelming majority of the people as the starting point and objective of all its work, constantly solve the most pressing and practical problems that are of the greatest concern to the people and affect their interests, and strive to enable the people to live a better life. Our goal is to satisfy the people's yearning for a better life.

—Excerpt from speeches during an inspection tour in Guangdong, December 7–11, 2012

The Chinese Dream is in the end the dream of the people, so we must rely closely on them to realize it and we must bring them constant benefits.

...

We must uphold the unity of the leadership of the CPC, the position of the people as masters of the country, and the rule of law; maintain the dominant position of the people; expand people's democracy; and promote the rule of law. We need to adhere to and improve the system of people's congresses as the fundamental political system, and the basic political systems of multiparty cooperation and political consultation under the leadership of the CPC, of regional ethnic autonomy, and of community-level self-governance. We need to build a service-oriented, accountable, law-based, and clean government; and give free rein to the people's enthusiasm.

...

We need to uphold the strategic thinking that development is the absolute principle and steadfastly take economic development as the central task. We need to comprehensively advance socialist economic, political, cultural, social, and ecological progress; deepen reform and opening up; give impetus to developing in a scientific manner; and continue to lay a solid material and cultural foundation for realizing the Chinese Dream.

...

We should always listen to the voice of the people and respond to their expectations, ensure their equal rights to participate in governance and develop themselves, and safeguard social fairness and justice. We need to make steady progress in ensuring that everyone wanting education can receive it, everyone needing a job can find one, everyone requiring medical care can receive it, everyone looking for affordable housing can find it, and everyone's last years are free from financial worry; and we need to constantly fulfill, safeguard, and develop the fundamental interests of the overwhelming majority of the people, so that everyone shares more fully and fairly in the fruits of development, and move steadily toward shared prosperity on the basis of constant economic and social development.

—Excerpts from a speech at the First Session of the Twelfth NPC, March 17, 2013

The mission of the CPC as China's ruling party is to lead the people in building a better country and improving their lives.

*—Answer to a question in a joint interview with
reporters from BRICS countries, March 19, 2013*

The Chinese working class should enhance its sense of historical mission and responsibility, and Chinese workers should be anchored in their jobs, bear in mind the overall situation, and purposefully integrate their life aspirations and the well-being of their families into the great cause of making the country prosperous and strong and rejuvenating the nation. They should closely link their personal dreams to the Chinese Dream, and constantly contribute to upholding and developing socialism with Chinese characteristics as the masters of the country.

*—Excerpt from a speech at the discussion session
with national model workers, April 28, 2013*

The Chinese Dream is the dream of the country and the nation but also of every Chinese person.

…

My young friends, I firmly believe that if the people of all our country's ethnic groups closely unite under the Party's leadership, keep their feet firmly planted on solid ground and forge ahead in a pioneering spirit, we can certainly build a prosperous, strong, democratic, culturally advanced, and harmonious modern socialist country by the middle of the century; and all our young people will surely witness and share in the realization of the Chinese Dream along with the people of all our country's ethnic groups.

—Excerpts from a speech to outstanding young people from all walks of life, May 4, 2013

Finishing building a moderately prosperous society in all respects, promoting socialist modernization and achieving the great rejuvenation of the Chinese nation are a glorious and great cause with a bright and splendid future. Everyone who dedicates themselves to this great cause can accomplish much. The great progress hundreds of millions of Chinese people are making presents Chinese students studying abroad with the opportunity to make innovations and realize their dreams. Students studying overseas should integrate their love of the country, their aspiration to make it strong and their efforts to serve it. They should merge their dreams into the extraordinary efforts of the people to realize the Chinese Dream and inscribe their names in the annals of the great rejuvenation of the Chinese nation.

—Excerpt from a speech at the centenary celebration event of the Western Returned Scholars Association, October 21, 2013

III

TO REALIZE THE CHINESE DREAM, WE MUST FOLLOW THE CHINESE PATH

Socialism with Chinese characteristics embodies the ideals and explorations of several generations of Chinese Communists, the aspirations and expectations of countless people with lofty ideals, the struggles and sacrifices of innumerable revolutionary martyrs, and the endeavors of people of all China's ethnic groups. It is the inevitable path China's social development took in modern times, and it is the choice of both history and the people. The great praxis of socialism with Chinese characteristics has not only made our country develop rapidly, our people's living standards improve quickly and the Chinese nation make great strides in catching up with contemporary trends and in creating bright prospects for its great rejuvenation, but has also made it possible for the Chinese people and nation to make a major contribution to world peace and development. Facts incontrovertibly prove that if we are to develop China, maintain its stability, finish building a moderately prosperous society in all respects, accelerate socialist modernization, and achieve the great rejuvenation of the Chinese nation, we must unswervingly uphold and develop socialism with Chinese characteristics.

—Excerpt from "The Six Areas of Work We Must Focus on to Fully Implement the Guiding Principles of the Eighteenth National Party Congress" (November 15, 2012), published in the journal Qiushi, *No. 1, 2013*

The long experience of the Party and the country fully confirms that only socialism can save China and only socialism with Chinese characteristics can develop China. Only by holding high the great banner of socialism with Chinese characteristics can we rally and lead the whole Party and the people of all our country's ethnic groups in finishing building a moderately prosperous society in all respects by the time the CPC celebrates its centenary and build China into a modern socialist country that is prosperous, strong, democratic, culturally advanced, and harmonious by the time the People's Republic of China marks its centenary, thereby winning an even brighter future for the Chinese people and nation.

...

Experience fully confirms that socialism with Chinese characteristics is a banner of the unity, progress, and success of the CPC and the Chinese people. We must always hold high this great banner and unwaveringly adhere to and develop socialism with Chinese characteristics in order to finish building a moderately prosperous society in all respects, accelerate socialist modernization, and achieve the great rejuvenation of the Chinese nation.

...

The path of socialism with Chinese characteristics is the only way to achieve China's socialist modernization and create a better life for the people. This path both takes economic development as the central task and comprehensively advances economic, political, cultural, social, and ecological progress as well as other aspects of progress; adheres to both the Four Cardinal Principles and the reform and opening up policy; and seeks both to further release and develop the productive forces, and to progressively achieve prosperity for all and promote well-rounded development of everyone.

—*Excerpts from "Focusing on Adhering to and Developing Socialism with Chinese Characteristics in Studying, Propagating and Implementing the Guiding Principles of the Eighteenth National Party Congress" (November 17, 2012), published in the* People's Daily *on November 19, 2012*

The Chinese nation today is one which is undergoing great changes. Since the introduction of the reform and opening up policy, we have reviewed our historical experience and constantly made difficult explorations, and we have finally found the right path to achieve the great rejuvenation of the Chinese nation and our achievements have attracted the world's attention. This path is socialism with Chinese characteristics.

...

With regard to the past, all Party members must bear in mind that backwardness leaves us vulnerable to attack whereas development makes us strong. With regard to the present, all Party members must bear in mind that the path we take determines our destiny and that finding the right path was not easy. We must unswervingly keep to it. With regard to the future, all Party members must bear in mind that we still have a long way to go and much hard work to do before our blueprint becomes a reality.

—Excerpts from a speech at the exhibition "The Road of Rejuvenation," November 29, 2012

Reform and opening up was a historical milestone that marked a great awakening of the Party. It has given birth to great innovations in both theory and praxis in the new era. China's development has proved the wisdom and correctness of the reform and opening up policy adopted by the Party under the guidance of Deng Xiaoping. He truly deserves to be called the chief architect of China's reform and opening up as well as the initiator of the path of socialism with Chinese characteristics. In the future, we must keep to this correct path which strengthens the country and enriches the people. We should not only keep to this path, but also take new steps to improve it.

—Excerpt from speeches during an inspection tour in Guangdong, December 7–11, 2012

Orientation determines the path, and the path determines destiny. What is most important for the great success of China's reform and opening up is that we take the Party's basic line as the lifeline of the Party and country. In building socialism with Chinese characteristics, we have always integrated keeping economic development as the central task with adhering to the two basic points of upholding the Four Cardinal Principles and carrying out reform and opening up. We have rejected both the old and rigid closed-door policy and any attempt to abandon socialism and take an erroneous path.

—Excerpt from a speech at the Second Group Study Session of the Political Bureau of the Eighteenth CPC Central Committee, December 31, 2012

Socialism with Chinese characteristics is the fundamental achievement of the Party and the people's 90-plus years of struggle, creation and accumulation and the fundamental crystallization of more than 30 years of reform and opening up. It encapsulates the dream of realizing the great rejuvenation of the Chinese nation, the most fundamental dream of the Chinese people throughout modern times, and embodies humanity's yearning for and tireless exploration of socialism in the modern age.

...

We firmly believe that as socialism with Chinese characteristics constantly develops, our system will certainly mature, the superiority of China's socialist system will surely become more evident, our path will inevitably become wider and the influence of China's development path on the world will constantly increase. We must have such confidence in our path, theory and system to truly measure up to these famous lines: "In spite of all beats, it stands still, not bending low. Whether from east, west, south or north the wind does blow."

...

In the historical periods of revolution, construction and reform, our Party proceeded from China's national conditions in exploring and forming the path of the new-democratic revolution, the path of socialist transformation and socialist construction, and the path of socialism with Chinese characteristics in line with China's reality. This independent and self-reliant spirit of exploration and this firm resolve to take our own path are the essence of the Party's constant awakening from setbacks and constant advance from victory to victory. Mr. Lu Xun famously said: At first there were no roads, but when many people walked the same way, roads came into being. Socialism with Chinese characteristics is the dialectical unity of the theoretical logic of scientific socialism and historical logic of China's social development. It is scientific socialism rooted in the land of China, reflected in the wishes of the Chinese people and adapted to the development and progress of China and the times. And it is the road we must follow to finish building a moderately prosperous society in all respects, accelerate socialist modernization and achieve the great rejuvenation of the Chinese nation. As long as we take our own path independently, rely only on ourselves, and unswervingly adhere to and develop socialism with Chinese characteristics, we can certainly finish building a moderately prosperous society in all respects by the centenary of the founding of the CPC, and finish building a prosperous, democratic, culturally advanced and harmonious modern socialist country by the centenary of the founding of New China.

—Excerpts from a speech at a seminar for new members and alternate members of the CPC Central Committee on the study and implementation of the guiding principles of the Eighteenth National Party Congress, January 5, 2013

China must take its own path to realize the Chinese Dream. This is the path of socialism with Chinese characteristics. This hard-won path came from more than 30 years of great experience in reform and opening up, continuous explorations in the 60-plus years of the People's Republic of China, a thorough review of the Chinese nation's development in its 170-plus-year modern history, and the inheritance of Chinese civilization through more than 5,000 years. This path is deeply rooted in history and broadly based on China's present realities. The Chinese nation has extraordinary creativity with which it has created our great Chinese civilization, and we can also expand and continue on the development path suitable to China's own conditions. The people of all ethnic groups throughout the country must strengthen their confidence in the theory, path and system of socialism with Chinese characteristics and steadfastly and courageously forge ahead along the correct Chinese path.

—Excerpt from a speech at the First Session of the Twelfth NPC, March 17, 2013

The world is changing and so is China. Socialism with Chinese characteristics must also move forward in keeping with the changing circumstances and conditions. China can remain vibrant only by constantly advancing with the times. We are willing to learn from the fine achievements of all civilizations, but we will not slavishly copy the development model of any other country. China's reform is about the self-improvement and self-development of the socialist system with Chinese characteristics. The only path that will ultimately take us far and guide us to success is the one that is chosen by the Chinese people and suited to China's reality.

—Answer to a question in a joint interview with reporters from BRICS countries, March 19, 2013

Socialism with Chinese characteristics is the fundamental orientation for the development and progress of contemporary China. It is the only way to realize the Chinese Dream and to guide our country's working class toward a brighter future.

—Excerpt from a speech at the discussion session with national model workers, April 28, 2013

To realize the Chinese Dream, we must adhere to the path of socialism with Chinese characteristics. We have taken this path for over 30 years now, and history has shown us that this correct path suits China's national conditions, enriches its people, and strengthens the country. We will unswervingly continue down this path.

—Answer to a question in a joint interview with reporters from Trinidad and Tobago, Costa Rica and Mexico, May 2013

The path we take, whether in revolution, construction or reform, is the most fundamental issue.

...

The fundamental reason we have achieved development over the past 30-plus years that is unprecedented in human history is that our path is correct. What is most important now is that we unwaveringly keep to our path of socialism with Chinese characteristics, and broaden and extend it as we progress with the times.

...

The path of socialism with Chinese characteristics, the theoretical system of socialism with Chinese characteristics and the socialist system with Chinese characteristics are the products of the long-term struggle of the whole Party and the people of all ethnic groups across the country, and they have all been proven to be scientific by long-term practice. Our confidence in this path, theory and system comes from practice, the people and truth.

—Excerpts from a speech at the Seventh Group Study Session of the Political Bureau of the Eighteenth CPC Central Committee, June 25, 2013

IV

TO REALIZE THE CHINESE DREAM, WE MUST FOSTER THE CHINESE SPIRIT

The Chinese nation has a history of more than 5,000 years of civilization and has created and passed on rich and outstanding cultural traditions. On the one hand, as practice develops and society advances, we will create an even more advanced culture; and on the other hand, the outstanding cultural traditions we have accumulated throughout our history will never become outmoded with the passage of time. We must not discard the fine cultural traditions of the Chinese nation; on the contrary, we must carry them on because they are the base and the soul of the Chinese nation, and if our nation loses its base and soul it will be without a foundation.

...

The Chinese nation possesses a spirit of perseverance, rejuvenation and tenacity. Especially since modern times, people with lofty ideals of one generation after another were not hesitant to shed blood or lay down their lives in order to change the semi-colonial and semi-feudal status of China and achieve the independence of the nation and the liberation of its people because they relied on a belief and made it into an ideal. Although they knew they would never achieve their own ideals, they firmly believed that their lofty ideals would ultimately be achieved with the continued efforts and sacrifices of generations to come.

—Excerpts from speeches during an inspection tour in Guangdong, December 7–11, 2012

China's traditional culture is both extensive and profound, and studying and grasping the essence of its various ideas is very beneficial for establishing a correct worldview, outlook on life and sense of values. The ancients said we should have the political aspiration of "being the first to worry about the world's troubles and the last to enjoy its pleasures"; the patriotic feelings of "not daring to ignore the country's peril no matter how humble one's position is" and "doing everything possible to save the country in its peril without regard to personal fortune or misfortune"; the uprightness of "never being corrupted by riches and honors, never departing from principle despite poverty or humble origin, and never submitting to force or threat"; and the selfless dedication to "die with a loyal heart shining in the pages of history" and "give one's all till one's heart ceases to beat." These sayings reflect the outstanding traditional culture and the spirit of the Chinese nation, and we all should keep them alive and foster them.

—Excerpt from a speech at the Celebration Assembly of the 80th Anniversary of the Central Party School and the Opening Ceremony of Its 2013 Spring Semester, March 1, 2013

We need to greatly strengthen the cultivation of ideology and ethics. The deep conviction, loving heart, selfless spirit and enterprising spirit that Lei Feng, Guo

Mingyi and Luo Yang had are the best portrayal of our national spirit. These three men are the backbone of our nation. We need to make full use of the examples of our country's heroes, greatly encourage the positive energy of society, and provide a powerful inner force for realizing the Chinese Dream.

—Excerpt from a speech to the Liaoning Delegation to the First Session of the Twelfth NPC, March 6, 2013

The Chinese nation has an unbroken history of more than 5,000 years of civilization. It has created a culture that is both extensive and profound and has made an indelible contribution to the progress of human civilization. After thousands of years of vicissitudes, the 56 ethnic groups of China's 1.3 billion-plus people are closely united because of our common extraordinary struggle, the beautiful homeland we have built together, and the national spirit we have cultivated together. But running through it all and what is most important are the ideals and convictions that we share and firmly hold to.

...

To realize the Chinese Dream, we must foster the Chinese spirit. This is the national spirit that has patriotism at its core and the spirit of the times that has reform and innovation at its core. This spirit rallies the people and pools their strength and it is the basis for reviving and strengthening the country. Patriotism has always been the inner force that binds the Chinese nation, and reform and innovation have always been the inner force that spurs us to keep up with the times in reform and opening up. The people of all ethnic groups must foster the great national spirit and the spirit of the times, constantly strengthen their inner bond of unity and motivation for self-improvement, and always vigorously march into the future.

—Excerpts from a speech at the First Session of the Twelfth NPC, March 17, 2013

Since the founding of New China, a large number of advanced role models—such as Meng Tai, the steel mill guard who would sleep in the blast furnace; Wang Jinxi, the Daqing Oilfield worker known as "Iron Man"; Deng Jiaxian, the physicist who developed China's atomic and nuclear bombs; Jiang Zhuying, the eminent scientist who died of exhaustion due to overwork; and Shi Chuanxiang, who said "It is worth one person getting dirty if it helps a thousand people get clean"—responded to the Party's call and led the people in becoming self-reliant and making the country strong. Wang Jinxi had the noble character to say, "I am willing to shorten my life by 20 years to open up this oilfield," and he led his oil-drilling team in an all-out struggle against nature for the development of China's oil industry. The Iron Man Spirit and the Daqing Oilfield Spirit inspired the people of all our ethnic groups to throw themselves wholeheartedly into socialist construction.

...

We must consciously put into practice core socialist values, carry forward the great character of our country's working class, and use advanced ideas and exemplary action to influence and lead the whole society, constantly infuse new energy into the Chinese spirit and always be a model for fostering the Chinese spirit.

...

Energetic efforts must be made to promote the spirit of model workers. The power of a good example is endless. Model workers are elite members of the nation and role models for the people. For a long time, model workers have made extraordinary achievements through ordinary work; forged the model worker spirit of "being dedicated to their work and striving for excellence, working hard and boldly innovating, and being indifferent to fame and wealth, and willing to make sacrifices"; and enriched the content of the national spirit and spirit of the times. This is our invaluable intellectual wealth.

...

To achieve our development goals, we must not only strengthen ourselves materially but also culturally and ethically. The people of all our ethnic groups should learn from model workers, follow their examples, make full use of their time, and work together to achieve the grand cause of the great rejuvenation of the Chinese nation.

*—Excerpts from a speech at the discussion session
with national model workers, April 28, 2013*

Ideals provide direction in life and faith determines the success or failure of a cause. Without ideals and convictions one's spirit becomes weak. The Chinese Dream is the common ideal of people of all China's ethnic groups, and a lofty, broad ideal that young people should firmly establish. Socialism with Chinese characteristics is the correct path for leading the people to realize the Chinese Dream that the Party articulated after untold hardships, and all young people should firmly adopt it to guide their lives.

...

Innovation is the soul driving a nation's progress and an inexhaustible source of a country's prosperity. It is also an essential part of the Chinese national character. This is what Confucius meant when he said, "If you can one day renovate yourself, do so from day to day. Yea, let there be daily renovation." Life never favors those who explore the beaten track and are satisfied with the status quo, and it never waits for the unambitious and those who sit idle and enjoy the fruits of others' work. Instead, it provides more opportunities to those who have the ability and courage to innovate.

...

Young people should dare to be the first, boldly emancipate their minds and progress with the times, dare to seek high and low for a way to forge ahead, and be ambitious to learn from and then surpass the generation before them. When young, they should create a young country and a young nation. Young people should have the willpower to cut paths through mountains and build bridges over rivers, and be indomitable and advance bravely in bringing forth new ideas. They should have a pragmatic attitude that demands truth so they can constantly accumulate experience and achieve results in the course of bringing forth new ideas in their chosen occupations.

...

Our country and our nation have progressed step by step from being poor and weak to being developed and prosperous today by relying on the tenacity of one generation after another and by relying on the Chinese nation's spirit of constant self-improvement through hard work.

...

Socialism with Chinese characteristics is a form of socialism in which material progress and cultural and ethical progress go hand in hand. It is difficult for a nation without inner strength to be self-reliant, and a cause that lacks a cultural buttress cannot be sustained for a long time.

—*Excerpts from a speech to outstanding young people from all walks of life, May 4, 2013*

To realize the Chinese Dream, we must carry forward the Chinese spirit. We need to use the national spirit centered on patriotism and spirit of the times centered on reform and innovation to rouse the energy and spirit of the whole nation.

—Answer to a question in a joint interview with reporters from Trinidad and Tobago, Costa Rica and Mexico, May 2013

Having strong patriotic feelings is the first requirement for our country's scientists and engineers. Science knows no borders, but scientists have a motherland. Scientists and engineers should strive to make scientific and technological innovations, serve the country and bring benefits to the people; apply their scientific and technological achievements to the great cause of making China a modern country; and integrate their goals in life with the effort to realize the Chinese Dream of the great rejuvenation of the Chinese nation.

—Excerpt from a speech during an inspection tour at the Chinese Academy of Sciences, July 17, 2013

The successes of the manned spaceflight program fully testify to the greatness of China's path, spirit and power. These successes have strengthened the determination and confidence with which the people of all our country's ethnic groups pursue the Chinese Dream of the great rejuvenation of the Chinese nation.

—Excerpt from a speech at a meeting with astronauts of the Shenzhou 10 manned spaceflight and people who worked on the program, July 26, 2013

Comrade Lan Hui always gave the cause of the Party and the people a special place in his heart. He was a good official who used his life to carry out the Party's mass line and was a model Communist for our times. Party members and officials should learn from his political character of firm conviction and loyalty to the Party, his public-service attitude of caring for the people and fulfilling his responsibilities to them, his professional spirit of working selflessly and progressing pragmatically, and his noble character of placing public interests above personal interests and daring to take on responsibility. They should become firmly aware that the Party's purpose is to serve the people wholeheartedly, willingly serve the people pragmatically and honestly, better play an exemplary role, and constantly make tangible achievements that can be put into practice, satisfy the people and withstand the test of time.

—Excerpt from instructions regarding Lan Hui's good work in carrying out the Party's mass line, September 22, 2013

Paragons of morality are important banners for building public morals. We need to carry out in-depth activities to learn from and publicize paragons of morality, foster truth, goodness and beauty, and spread positive energy. We should inspire the people to esteem virtue, perform good deeds, and emulate virtuous people. And we should encourage the whole society to cultivate morality by practicing goodness and to exert a positive influence through ethical behavior. In this way, we will create a strong spirit and powerful ethical support for realizing the Chinese Dream of the great rejuvenation of the Chinese nation.

...

Inner strength is limitless, as is moral strength. Chinese civilization has a long history stretching back to antiquity, and it gave birth to the precious inner character of the Chinese nation and cultivated the Chinese people's pursuit of noble values. The thinking of constant self-improvement and embracing the world through virtue supports the Chinese nation's ceaseless self-regeneration, and today it is still a powerful motivation for carrying out reform and opening up and for socialist modernization.

—Excerpts from a speech to the fourth group of nominees and recipients of national morality model awards, September 26, 2013

In the long history of the Chinese nation, which stretches continuously for thousands of years, patriotism has always been the stirring theme and a powerful force inspiring the people of our country's ethnic groups to constantly make improvements. No matter how long the shadow a tree casts, its roots are ever in the soil. No matter where they study, Chinese students should always keep the motherland and its people in their hearts.

...

I hope that Chinese students studying abroad draw upon and carry forward the glorious tradition of serving the country while abroad, be an adherer to and communicator of patriotism, uphold the ideal of "being the first to worry about the world's troubles and the last to enjoy its pleasures," always aspire to strive to make the country prosperous and strong, the nation energetic and the people happy, and willingly attach the fruits of their personal successes to the evergreen tree of patriotism.

—Excerpts from a speech at the centenary celebration event of the Western Returned Scholars Association, October 21, 2013

V

TO REALIZE THE CHINESE DREAM, WE MUST COALESCE CHINA'S STRENGTH

The people are the creators of history; they are the real heroes. The people are the source of our strength. We are very aware that the capability of any individual is limited, but as long as we unite as one like a fortress, there is no difficulty we cannot overcome.

—Excerpt from a speech at a press conference held by the members of the Standing Committee of the Political Bureau of the Eighteenth CPC Central Committee, November 15, 2012

If our 1.3 billion citizens and 82 million Party members as well as overseas Chinese can achieve consensus, we will constitute a powerful force. At the same time, we must realize that people from different localities and social strata who have different backgrounds and occupations think differently. We must therefore consider: Where can we find common ground? In what areas can we work to achieve consensus? Where can we allow differences to persist? We need to find the greatest common divisor and use it as the focus for reform and opening up so that we can accomplish twice as much with half the effort. Sharpening the axe will not interfere with the cutting of firewood. Preparatory work must be done. One must not worry about it taking too long, for the work will be accomplished in the fullness of time. This includes carrying out trials beforehand, which can also solve problems of understanding. We need to respect people's creativity, pool their wisdom to the greatest extent possible, broadly unite with all possible forces inside and outside the Party, fully mobilize all possible positive factors at home and abroad, and coalesce them into a powerful force to carry out reform and opening up.

—Excerpt from speeches during an inspection tour in Guangdong, December 7–11, 2012

Reform and opening up are a cause hundreds of millions of people are directly engaged in. We must continue to respect their pioneering spirit and carry out the cause under the Party's leadership. Reform and opening up are a unity of what the people demand and the Party espouses. The people are the creators of history and carry out the cause of reform and opening up. Therefore, we must steadfastly integrate the dominant position of the people with the leadership of the Party and rely closely on the people in promoting reform and opening up. Every breakthrough and development in understanding and practice in reform and opening up, the production and development of every new thing in the course of reform and opening up, and the creation and accumulation of every new experience gained in reform and opening up all derive from the experience and wisdom of our hundreds of millions of people.

...

The more arduous the tasks of reform, development and stability, the more we should strengthen and improve the Party's leadership and the more we need to maintain the Party's intimate ties with the people. We need to excel at leading the people forward by proposing and implementing the correct line, principles and policies, and we need to excel at improving our policies on the basis of the people's creations from practice and their requirements of development. We need to ensure that all the people receive more of the fruits of reform and development and share in them more equitably, and continue to reinforce the popular support for the deepening of reform and opening up.

—Excerpts from a speech at the Second Group Study Session of the Political Bureau of the Eighteenth CPC Central Committee, December 31, 2012

"Many hands make a bigger fire." The Eighteenth National Congress of the CPC made plans for consolidating and developing the broadest possible patriotic united front, and gave the Chinese People's Political Consultative Conference (CPPCC) greater responsibilities and a more glorious mission. All political parties, people's organizations and individuals from all ethnic groups and all walks of life in the CPPCC need to conscientiously align their thinking and action with the guidelines of the Eighteenth National Congress; uphold and improve the system of multiparty cooperation and political consultation under the leadership of the CPC; ensure the CPPCC fully plays its important role of coordinating relations, pooling strength, making proposals and serving the overall situation; promote harmony in relations between political parties, between ethnic groups, between religious groups, between social strata, and between our compatriots at home and abroad; and mobilize all positive factors to the greatest possible extent to work together to achieve the great rejuvenation of the Chinese nation.

...

The cause of socialism with Chinese characteristics is both a glorious cause that benefits the people and a difficult cause that requires all our wisdom and strength. We have already sounded the call for finishing building a moderately prosperous society in all respects, but the key to accomplishing this is to be fully confident we can solve remaining tough problems, coalesce a powerful force to carry the cause forward, closely rely on all our country's ethnic groups, and spur the Party and country's cause from one success to another.

—Excerpts from a speech at a New Year's tea party held by the CPPCC National Committee, January 1, 2013

We need to build the ranks of scientists and engineers, provide them with greater opportunities to put their talent to best use, and encourage them to contribute their wisdom and strength to the great goal of realizing the Chinese Dream.

> *—Excerpt from a speech to the members of the CPPCC National Committee from the China Association for Science and Technology and China's scientific and technological community participating in the First Session of the Twelfth CPPCC National Committee, March 4, 2013*

To realize the Chinese Dream, we must coalesce China's strength; that is, the strength of the great unity among the people of all our ethnic groups. The Chinese Dream is the dream of our nation and of every Chinese. As long as we are united closely in the struggle to fulfill this common dream, the strength to achieve it will be so overwhelming that each one of us will have more room to achieve our own dreams. The Chinese people who live in our great motherland in this great age all share the opportunity to accomplish something great in their lives, share the opportunity to make their dreams come true, and share the opportunity to grow and progress along with the motherland and the times. With a dream, opportunity and effort, all beautiful things can be created. The people of all our ethnic groups must bear their mission in mind and direct their thought and action to the same goal. We should coalesce the wisdom and strength of our country's 1.3 billion people into a majestic invincible force.

...

We need to consolidate and develop the broadest possible patriotic united front; strengthen the CPC's unity and cooperation with the democratic parties and public figures without party affiliation; consolidate and develop socialist ethnic relations of equality, unity, mutual assistance and harmony; make use of the positive role religious figures and believers play in promoting economic and social development; and do our utmost to unite with all possible forces.

...

Workers, farmers, and intellectuals across the country need to put their talents to full use, work diligently, and play the dominant role in economic and social development. All government employees need to serve public interests selflessly, work honestly and industriously, show concern for the people's suffering, and do practical work for them. All members of the People's Liberation Army and the People's Armed Police Force must act in accordance with the purpose of having a strong army that follows the commands of the CPC, is capable of winning battles, and has a fine work style; become better able to perform their missions; resolutely defend national sovereignty, security, and development interests; and resolutely protect the lives and property of the people. All persons working in the non-public sector of the economy and those from new social strata need to promote the creativity and entrepreneurship of labor, give back to society, bring benefits to the people, and become qualified builders of socialism with Chinese characteristics. The nation's youth should aim high, learn more knowledge, temper their will, and let their formative years radiate brilliantly in the progress of the times.

—Excerpts from a speech at the First Session of the Twelfth NPC, March 17, 2013

For now and a period of time in the future, a major task of strengthening the military ideologically and politically is to educate and guide officers and enlisted personnel to keep in mind the purpose of having a strong military, strive to integrate their personal ambitions with the dream of having a strong military, strengthen their sense of mission, and vow to be firmly rooted in the military and to achieve success through their service.

—Excerpt from a speech during an inspection tour of the naval base in Sanya, April 9, 2013

We must give full play to the dominant role of the working class. The working class is our country's leading class. It represents our country's advanced productive forces and relations of production, it is our Party's most steadfast and reliable class base, and it is the main force for finishing building a moderately prosperous society in all respects and upholding and developing socialism with Chinese characteristics.

...

The Chinese working class must adhere to the mission of rejuvenating China, give full play to its great creative power, carry forward its glorious tradition of knowing the big picture and considering the overall situation, consciously maintain political stability and unity, and always make up the nucleus that unites China's strength.

—*Excerpts from a speech at the discussion session with national model workers, April 28, 2013*

"Small affairs go smoothly only when they fit into a larger picture." You can accomplish something significant in your life only if you integrate your ambitions into the cause of your country and nation. I hope all of you cherish your youth and make the most of it, have the courage to advance in the front ranks of the times and be pioneers who make a contribution, strive to make yourselves useful in building the motherland, and contribute your wisdom and strength to realizing the Chinese Dream.

—*Excerpt from a reply letter to all members of the Class of 2013 Undergraduate Chinese Communist*

Youth League Branch at the Peking University School of Archeology and Museology, May 2, 2013

History and current events tell us that if our young people have ideals and the resolve to act on them, our country will have a future, our nation will have hope and we will have an inexhaustible supply of strength to achieve our development goals.

...

One can do well only when one's country and nation do well. Only if everyone fights for a better tomorrow can their efforts be aggregated into a powerful force to realize the Chinese Dream.

...

Looking to the future, we can see that our young generation has a promising future and they will accomplish much. It is a law of history that the waves of the Yangtze River from behind drive on those ahead, and it is the responsibility of young people to surpass their elders. Today's young people need to boldly assume the heavy responsibilities that the times impose on them, aim high, be practical and realistic, and put their youthful dreams into action in the course of realizing the Chinese Dream of the great rejuvenation of the Chinese nation.

...

The theme of the Chinese youth movement today is to strive to realize the Chinese Dream of the great rejuvenation of the Chinese nation. The Chinese Communist Youth League should carry out extensive educational and practical activities for our country's young people centered on the theme "My Chinese Dream." It should sow the seeds of and ignite the dreams of each youth so that more young people dare to dream and pursue their dreams and strive to fulfill them, and so that all young people increase their youthful energy to realize the Chinese Dream.

—Excerpts from a speech to outstanding young people from all walks of life, May 4, 2013

To realize the Chinese Dream, we must coalesce China's strength. Empty talk harms the country and hard work makes it flourish. We need to use the wisdom and strength of our country's 1.3 billion people and get generation after generation of Chinese to strive tirelessly to build a strong China and a prosperous nation.

—Answer to a question in a joint interview with reporters from Trinidad and Tobago, Costa Rica and Mexico, May 2013

If we are to realize the Chinese Dream and the goals set forth at the Party's Eighteenth National Congress, we must rely closely on the people and fully mobilize the enthusiasm, initiative and creativity of as many people as possible.

—Excerpt from a speech at a work conference on educational and practical activities pertaining to the Party's mass line, June 18, 2013

Achieving the goals and completing the tasks set forth at the Party's Eighteenth National Congress and achieving the great rejuvenation of the Chinese nation are the main tasks of the Party and country and the theme of the women's movement in present-day China. We need to firmly grasp this modern theme, intimately merge the course of China's development and progress with the course of promoting equal development of men and women, make the development of the Chinese women's cause more pertinent to the times, and give our country's hundreds of millions of women greater responsibilities to bear.

—Remark to the new leading body of the All-China Women's Federation, October 31, 2013

VI

CHINESE COMPATRIOTS EVERYWHERE SHOULD WORK TOGETHER TO REALIZE THE CHINESE DREAM OF THE GREAT REJUVENATION OF THE CHINESE NATION

Achieving the great rejuvenation of the Chinese nation has been the greatest dream of the Chinese people since modern times. I believe that our compatriots in Hong Kong also hold this dream dearly. I also believe that our Hong Kong compatriots, who have a deep sense of national respect and pride, will surely contribute along with all the people of the country to achieving the great rejuvenation of the Chinese nation.

—Excerpt from a discussion with Leung Chun-ying, chief executive of the Hong Kong Special Administrative Region, December 20, 2012

We are filled with confidence that, as we continue to unwaveringly promote the peaceful development of relations between the two sides of the Taiwan Straits, we will overcome all difficulties in opening up new prospects for these cross-Straits relations, and greet the great rejuvenation of the Chinese nation hand in hand with our Taiwan compatriots.

...

Although cross-Straits relations have had their ups and downs, it is finally possible to break the long-standing estrangement and begin exchanges and cooperation. This is because compatriots on both sides of the Straits are members of the Chinese nation, and these natural blood ties cannot be broken by any force; because both sides of the

Straits are part of the one and same China, and no force can change this basic fact; and because cross-Straits exchanges and cooperation are blessed with advantageous natural conditions, and no force can stifle this demand for two-way benefits. This is all the more because all sons and daughters of the Chinese nation are resolved to work tirelessly to stand tall among the world's nations, and no force can obstruct this common aspiration of the whole nation.

...

"When brothers stand together, they are invincible." Compatriots on both sides of the Straits must work together if we are to achieve the great rejuvenation of the Chinese nation. We sincerely hope that Taiwan and the mainland develop together, and compatriots on both sides of the Straits work together to realize the Chinese Dream. Promoting the peaceful development of cross-Straits relations hand in hand and achieving the great rejuvenation of the Chinese nation with one heart should become the theme of cross-Straits relations and the common mission of the Chinese people on both sides of the Straits.

—Excerpts from a discussion with Lien Chan, honorary chairman of the Chinese Kuomintang, and his delegation, February 25, 2013

Our compatriots in the special administrative regions of Hong Kong and Macao need to put the overall interests of the country and their regions first and work together with all Chinese to safeguard and promote lasting prosperity and stability in Hong Kong and Macao. Our compatriots in Taiwan and on the mainland need to join hands in supporting, maintaining, and promoting the peaceful development of cross-Straits relations, improving people's lives on both sides, and creating a new future for the Chinese nation. Overseas Chinese should carry forward the Chinese nation's fine traditions of diligence and kindheartedness, and strive to contribute to the development of the motherland and to friendship between Chinese nationals and the local people in their host countries.

—Excerpt from a speech at the First Session of the Twelfth NPC, March 17, 2013

We must steadfastly address the overall situation of cross-Straits relations in the overall interests of the Chinese nation. We will steadfastly safeguard the fundamental interests of the Chinese nation and the common interests of all sons and daughters of the Chinese nation, including our Taiwan compatriots. In addressing the overall situation of cross-Straits relations in the overall interests of the Chinese nation, what is most important is to safeguard the country's sovereignty and territorial integrity. Although the mainland and Taiwan have yet to be reunited, they are both part of the one and same China; that is, they are an indivisible whole.

The Kuomintang and the CPC should adhere to the one-China policy and uphold the one-China framework. I hope that both parties maintain a responsible attitude to history and the people, place the overall interests of the Chinese nation above all else, ensure the peaceful development of cross-Straits relations, and constantly advance cross-Straits relations in the right direction.

...

We must remain committed to the future of cross-Straits relations on the basis of a clear understanding of the trends of historical development. The great rejuvenation of the Chinese nation has brighter prospects now than ever before due to the tireless efforts of sons and daughters of the Chinese nation. We should have the foresight to see the great trends of the development of the times and the rejuvenation of our nation and to see that the peaceful development of cross-Straits relations has already become an important component of the great rejuvenation of the Chinese nation. We should cast off the shackles of old ideas that are ill-suited to the times and adopt common goals for rejuvenating China. The development of cross-Straits relations is the overall trend of events, and we should accordingly determine our own roadmap and continue to progress forward. Our two parties should take national rejuvenation and the people's happiness as our mission, promote unity and cooperation between compatriots on both sides of the Straits, actively propound the idea that we are one family, gather together the wisdom and strength of

Chinese people on both sides of the Straits, heal historical wounds in the course of working together to achieve the great rejuvenation of the Chinese nation, and write a new chapter in the nation's prosperity.

—Excerpts from a discussion with Wu Po-hsiung, honorary chairman of the Kuomintang, and his delegation, June 13, 2013

At present, cross-Straits relations stand at a new starting point and face an important opportunity. Our two parties should follow the trend of world development and conform to the rightness of benefiting the people on both sides of the Straits, have foresight, deepen mutual trust, interact beneficially, continue to promote the comprehensive development of cross-Straits relations, and widen the channels for the peaceful development of cross-Straits relations, so that cross-Straits relations continue to move forward, and we work together for the well-being of compatriots on both sides of the Straits and for the rejuvenation of the Chinese nation.

—Excerpt from a congratulatory message to Ma Ying-jeou, chairman of the Chinese Kuomintang, July 20, 2013

By striving to finish building a moderately prosperous society in all respects and achieve the great rejuvenation of the Chinese nation we are providing a broad stage upon which Chinese entrepreneurs can pursue their ambitions. We will further deepen reform, improve policies, and strengthen services; protect the rights and interests of Chinese entrepreneurs' investments and enterprises in accordance with the law; and encourage Chinese entrepreneurs to contribute their wisdom and energy to China's development and support them in doing so.

"I will mount a long wind some day and break the heavy waves and set my cloudy sail straight and bridge the deep, deep sea." I hope that Chinese entrepreneurs like all of you seize the opportunities available and make full use of your strengths, actively take an interest and participate in China's reform and opening up and its modernization, expand your undertakings by means of mutually beneficial cooperation, and make new and greater contributions to jointly realizing the Chinese Dream of the great rejuvenation of the Chinese nation and to promoting exchanges and cooperation between Chinese people and the peoples of other countries.

—Excerpt from the congratulatory letter to the Twelfth World Chinese Entrepreneurs Convention, September 25, 2013

Both sides of the Straits should keep to the correct path of peaceful development of cross-Straits relations, propound the idea that we are one family, strengthen exchanges and cooperation, and together promote the great rejuvenation of the Chinese nation.

—Excerpt from a discussion with Vincent Siew, honorary chairman of the Cross-Straits Common Market Foundation, and his delegation, October 6, 2013

VII

THE CHINESE DREAM IS A DREAM OF PEACE, DEVELOPMENT, COOPERATION AND MUTUAL BENEFIT

The Chinese nation is a peace-loving nation. Eliminating war and achieving peace has been the most urgent and deepest wish of the Chinese people throughout modern times. Taking the path of peaceful development is an extension and development of the Chinese nation's outstanding cultural traditions, and the inevitable conclusion of the Chinese people's bitter experience throughout modern times. The Chinese people have the hardships of war burned in their memories, and they pursue peace tirelessly and cherish peace and stability in life. The Chinese people fear upheaval, demand stability, and yearn for peace.

...

Our path of peaceful development was hard won. It has been gradually developed by the Party on the basis of painstaking exploration and constant practice since the founding of New China and particularly since reform and opening up. Our Party has always held high the banner of peace and never wavered in this. On the basis of long experience, we advanced and adhered to the Five Principles of Peaceful Coexistence, set forth and pursued an independent foreign policy of peace, made the solemn commitment to the world never to seek hegemony or engage in expansion and stressed that China will always be a staunch force safeguarding world peace. We must unswervingly adhere to these principles and never vacillate from them.

...

The Eighteenth National Party Congress set forth the Two Centenary Goals. We have also set forth the goal to realize the Chinese Dream of the great rejuvenation of the Chinese nation. To achieve these goals, we need a peaceful international environment. Without peace, neither China nor the world can develop smoothly, and without development, neither China nor the world can have lasting peace. We must grasp opportunities, concentrate on managing our own affairs well, make the country richer and stronger and the people more prosperous, and better take the path of peaceful development by relying on the strength we derive from constant development.

...

We should keep to the path of peaceful development, but we must not relinquish our legitimate rights and interests or sacrifice our country's core interests. No foreign country should expect us to sell off our core interests, or to accept damage to our sovereignty, security or development interests. China is taking the path of peaceful development, as should other countries. Only in this way can countries develop together and coexist in peace.

—Excerpts from a speech at the Third Group Study Session of the Political Bureau of the Eighteenth CPC Central Committee, January 28, 2013

Chinese are peace-loving people. We will hold high the banner of peace, development, cooperation and mutual benefit; unwaveringly take the path of peaceful development;

unwaveringly follow a win-win strategy of opening up; be committed to developing friendship and cooperation with other countries; fulfill our international responsibilities and obligations; and continue to work with the peoples of all other countries in promoting the lofty cause of peace and development of humankind.

—Excerpt from a speech at the First Session of the Twelfth NPC, March 17, 2013

During more than 30 years of reform and opening up, China has achieved substantial progress in economic and social development and the people's lives have improved significantly. This is good for both China and the world. Chinese people are patriotic, yet also have global vision and an international perspective. As its strength grows, China will assume more international responsibilities and obligations within its capacity and make greater contributions to the noble cause of world peace and development.

...

Although China is the world's second-largest economy, its per capita GDP remains much lower than the world average and China still has a long way to go before our people are enriched and our country is made strong. Right now, some in the international community worry that once developed, China will seek hegemony and bully others. Such concerns are totally unnecessary. China has repeatedly made the solemn commitment to the international community that China will unswervingly follow the path of peaceful development and will never seek hegemony or expansion. We have a saying: "A word can never be withdrawn." We mean what we say and events already show that China does what it says it will do. We also hope that all other countries will take the path of peaceful development and make joint efforts to promote world peace and development.

...

Chinese people have valued harmony without sameness since ancient times. We hope that different countries and different civilizations will carry out exchanges on an equal footing, learn from each other and achieve common progress; that the people of all countries can share in the fruits of global economic, scientific and technological advances and have their wishes respected; and that all countries can make united efforts to promote the building of a harmonious world of enduring peace and shared prosperity.

—Excerpts from answer to a question in a joint interview with reporters from BRICS countries, March 19, 2013

China's development is inseparable from the world and from Africa. Prosperity and stability in Africa and the world also need China. Although there is a vast ocean separating

China and Africa, our hearts are connected. We are bound together not only by our deep traditional friendship and intertwined interests, but also by our own dreams.

The more than 1.3 billion Chinese are committed to realizing the Chinese Dream of the great rejuvenation of the Chinese nation, and the over one billion Africans are committed to realizing the African dream of gaining strength from unity and achieving development and revival. The people of China and Africa should strengthen unity and cooperation and enhance mutual support and assistance to achieve our dreams. We should also work together with the international community in realizing the worldwide dream of enduring peace and shared prosperity, and make new and even greater contributions to the noble cause of world peace and development.

—Excerpt from the speech "Trustworthy Friends and Sincere Partners Forever," at the Julius Nyerere International Convention Center, Tanzania, March 25, 2013

No matter how the international situation may change, we should always pursue peaceful development and win-win cooperation; desire peace, not war; seek cooperation instead of confrontation; and in the pursuit of national interests, take into consideration the legitimate concerns of other countries.

—Excerpt from the keynote speech "Work Hand in Hand for Common Development," at the Fifth BRICS Leaders Meeting, March 27, 2013

Peace is the eternal hope of the people. Like air and sunshine, people hardly notice peace when they have it, but life without it is impossible. Without peace, development is out of the question.

...

Countries, whether big or small, strong or weak, rich or poor, should be defenders and promoters of peace. Rather than undercutting each other's efforts, countries should complement each other and work for joint progress. The international community should advocate the vision of integrated security, shared security and cooperative security so that our global village becomes a major stage on which we can develop together, rather than an arena in which we wrestle with each other; or even worse, a region or the whole world is thrown into chaos to further someone's personal agenda.

—Excerpts from the keynote speech "Working Together toward a Better Future for Asia and the World," at the Boao Forum for Asia Annual Conference 2013, April 7, 2013

To realize the Chinese Dream, we must pursue peaceful development. We will always unwaveringly follow the path of peaceful development and unswervingly pursue an opening up strategy that brings mutual benefit. We will concentrate on both China's development and our responsibilities and contributions to the world. We will bring benefit to both the Chinese people and the people of the world. The realization of the Chinese Dream will bring the world peace, not turmoil; opportunities, not menace.

...

Although there is a vast ocean between China and Latin America, our hearts are connected. We are bound together not only by our profound traditional friendship and close interests, but also by our common pursuit of beautiful dreams.

In recent years, Latin American and Caribbean countries have made steady progress in achieving common development through joint efforts. The establishment of the Community of Latin American and Caribbean States fully testifies to the vigorous efforts made by Latin America to realize the dream of unity, coordination and common development championed by the pioneers of the Latin American independence movements.

China is ready to work with Latin American and Caribbean countries hand in hand, supporting one another and cooperating sincerely on the path to realize the great dream of development and prosperity.

—Excerpts from answer to a question in a joint interview with reporters from Trinidad and Tobago, Costa Rica and Mexico, May 2013

I made it clear to President Obama that China will unwaveringly take the path of peaceful development, unwaveringly deepen reform and expand opening up, strive to realize the Chinese Dream of the great rejuvenation of the Chinese nation, and promote humanity's noble cause of peace and development.

The Chinese Dream seeks to make the country prosperous and strong, rejuvenate the nation and make the people happy. This is a dream of peace, development, cooperation and mutual benefit, and it is closely linked to the dreams of the people of the world, including the United States.

...

President Obama and I both believe that, faced with the rapid development of economic globalization and the objective needs of the countries in the same boat, China and the United States should take, and are capable of taking, a new and different way in order to avoid the great power conflicts and confrontations of the past. Both sides agree that we should strive together to build a new kind of relations among major powers, respect each other, cooperate to our mutual advantage, and bring benefits to our people and to the people of the whole world. The international community is also looking forward to constantly improved and developed Sino-US relations. If China and the United States cooperate well, they can be the anchor of world stability and the booster of world peace.

—Remark at a joint press conference held with US President Barack Obama, June 7, 2013

China has set forth the Two Centenary Goals as a grand blueprint for its future development. China needs the United Nations and the United Nations also needs China. China attaches great importance to the UN and will firmly support it. China is a permanent member of the UN Security Council. This is not only about power; it is a heavy responsibility that China readily undertakes. China will continue to promote the peaceful resolution of international disputes and support the UN in promoting the Millennium Development Goals. China is willing to work with all parties to address shared problems such as climate change, and to make greater contributions to world peace and human progress.

—Excerpt from a discussion with Ban Ki-moon, secretary-general of the UN, June 19, 2013

The Chinese Dream is closely linked with the pursuits and dreams of all ASEAN countries in their quest to develop and revitalize their countries and make their people prosperous and happy. China is willing to work with all ASEAN countries hand in hand with mutual understanding to achieve our ideals and to help each other, make the most of our respective strengths, uncover potential areas for cooperation and achieve mutual benefit.

—Answer to a question in a joint interview with Indonesian and Malaysian reporters, October 2013

China's development is inseparable from the world, and the world's development also needs China. China will unwaveringly take the path of peaceful development, unwaveringly follow an independent foreign policy of peace, and unwaveringly pursue an opening up strategy of mutual benefit. China's development is an outgrowth of peaceful forces in the world and represents positive energy for transmitting friendship. It brings development opportunities and not a threat to Asia and the world. China is willing to continue to share the opportunities for economic and social development with ASEAN, with Asia, and with the world.

—Excerpt from the speech "Hand in Hand Building a China-ASEAN Community of Shared Destiny," to the Indonesian Parliament, October 3, 2013

When we put forward the Chinese Dream of the great rejuvenation of the Chinese nation and stressed that the Chinese Dream is closely linked with the dreams of the people of our neighboring countries, many of their leaders responded positively. We need to strengthen communication, with the focus on bringing the Chinese Dream in accord with the wishes of the people of all our neighboring countries for a better life and with the outlook for regional development, and getting the thinking of a community of shared destiny to spread and take root in all our neighboring countries.

—Excerpt from a speech at a meeting on diplomatic work with neighboring countries, October 24, 2013

The Chinese people are hard at work trying to achieve the Two Centenary Goals and realize the Chinese Dream of the great rejuvenation of the Chinese nation. The Chinese Dream and the dreams of the Chinese people for a better life are connected, and also are linked to the beautiful dreams people in other countries have of peace and development.

—Comments made to foreign representatives at the 21st Century Council Beijing Conference, November 2, 2013

VIII

HARD WORK MAKES DREAMS
COME TRUE

The great rejuvenation of the Chinese nation along the path of socialism with Chinese characteristics is a noble cause with unparalleled glory that requires generation after generation of Chinese Communists to lead the people in continuous struggle. Today, the baton of history has been passed to us. History and the people have entrusted a heavy task to us and they both will judge our actions. The grand convictions of our Party have always been its strong ideological pillar, and the people have always been the foundation of our Party's governance. So long as we never waver in our convictions and never divorce ourselves from the people, we will be invincible. We, members of the Eighteenth Central Committee of the CPC, must not fail in our duty. We must remain loyal to the Party, to the country, and to the people, and draw on all our wisdom, strength, and thoughts and energies to deliver results that are worthy of history and the times and true to the expectations of the people.

> —*Excerpt from "The Six Areas of Work We Must Focus on to Fully Implement the Guiding Principles of the Party's Eighteenth National Congress" (November 15, 2012), published in the journal* Qiushi, *No. 1, 2013*

Achieving the great rejuvenation of the Chinese nation is a glorious and arduous undertaking that requires the common efforts of generation after generation of Chinese people. Empty talk harms the country and hard work makes it flourish. Our generation of Communists must inherit the past and set a new course for the future, do our Party building well, unite with all sons and daughters of the Chinese nation to build our country and develop our nation well, and continue to boldly advance toward the goal of the great rejuvenation of the Chinese nation.

—Excerpt from a speech at the exhibition "The Road of Rejuvenation," November 29, 2012

I want to again emphasize the slogan, "Empty talk harms the country and hard work makes it flourish." This resounding slogan was put forward by Comrade Deng Xiaoping during his inspection tour in southern China in 1992. Our country's more than 30 years of experience in carrying out reform and opening up has fully proved this truth. Looking toward tomorrow, we need to work hard to finish building a moderately prosperous society in all respects, to basically modernize China, and to achieve the great rejuvenation of the Chinese nation.

—Excerpt from speeches during an inspection tour in Guangdong, December 7–11, 2012

Empty talk harms the country and hard work makes it flourish. We all need to keep this principle firmly in mind. Leading officials at all levels need to steadfastly serve the people pragmatically and honestly, genuinely improve their work style, speak the truth and do useful things, make worthwhile accomplishments and boldly take on responsibility, and keep promises and be resolute in action.

...

"The value of a policy lies in the consistency of its application." In whatever official post we serve at the time, we must boldly carry out our work and forge ahead while maintaining overall stability and continuity in the work. We need to make adjustments and improvements where and when it is necessary, but we cannot start over every time there is a change of leadership; even more, we cannot set off in a new direction to display so-called achievements. Rather, we should genuinely implement a good blueprint to the end and earnestly accomplish something significant, not start over needlessly.

—Excerpts from a speech at the Central Economic Work Conference, December 15, 2012

We need to genuinely implement a good blueprint to the end and earnestly accomplish something significant. We need to proceed in the spirit of hammering nails. More often than not it takes more than one strike to hammer a nail. That is to say, achievement takes continuous effort and you cannot just stop in the middle of a job and leave it half done. We need to have the spirit of accomplishing a task without taking credit.

...

We need to have a correct conception of political accomplishments. We need to do work that builds a foundation and yields long-term benefits, and not engage in meaningless competition or undertake vanity projects that exhaust the people and waste money. We need to deal with concrete issues, do solid work, be willing to take on responsibility, and genuinely carry out our responsibilities to history and the people.

—Excerpts from a speech at the second meeting of the Second Plenary Session of the Eighteenth CPC Central Committee, February 28, 2013

All Party members, especially leading officials at all levels, need to have a sense of urgency that their skills are inadequate and they need to strive to improve them at every possible moment. We can accomplish the Two Centenary Goals and realize the Chinese Dream of the great rejuvenation of the Chinese nation only if all Party members constantly improve their skills.

—Excerpt from a speech at the Celebration Assembly of the 80th Anniversary of the Central Party School

and the Opening Ceremony of Its 2013 Spring
Semester, March 1, 2013

Faced with the mighty tide of the times and the great expectations of the people for a better life, we must not become complacent or indolent in the slightest. We must redouble our efforts and forge ahead relentlessly as we continue to carry forward the cause of socialism with Chinese characteristics, and struggle to realize the Chinese Dream of the great rejuvenation of the Chinese nation.

...

"One must have great ambition to achieve great exploits, and their achievement requires tireless effort." China is still in the primary stage of socialism and will remain so for a long time. There is still much to do and a long way to go before we can realize the Chinese Dream and create a better life for all our people, and every one of us has to continue working as hard as we can.

—Excerpts from a speech at the First Session of the
Twelfth NPC, March 17, 2013

People make history and labor creates the future. Labor is the fundamental force driving social progress. Happiness does not fall from the sky, and dreams do not come true automatically. To achieve our goals and create a bright future for ourselves, we must rely closely on the people and always act in their interests, and we must rely on industrious, honest and creative work. When we say, "Empty talk harms the country and hard work makes it flourish," we mean we must first and foremost work hard earnestly and practically.

...

We must continue to esteem labor and compensate laborers well. Labor is the source of wealth and happiness. People's beautiful dreams can be realized only through honest labor; all the difficulties that arise in the course of development can be solved only through honest labor; and everything in life that is glorious can be cast only through honest labor. Labor shaped the Chinese nation and its glorious history and it will shape its brilliant future as well. "There is nothing that cannot be accomplished through hard work." We must firmly adopt the thinking that labor is what is most honorable, most sublime, most excellent and most beautiful; and get all the people to have greater enthusiasm for labor and release their creative potential to create a better life through labor.

...

A journey of a thousand miles begins with a single step. There is a bright future for our country's development, but it will not be easy. We cannot accomplish our master plan in one single effort, and we cannot realize our dreams overnight. Everything in the world was hard won. The more beautiful the future, the harder we must work for it.

...

The only way to overcome difficulties and realize our dreams is by doing solid work. We need to make a great effort to foster the fine attitude of doing solid work and working hard throughout society. Leading officials at all levels should foster the spirit of model workers; and make realistic plans, encourage genuine enthusiasm and handle things in a practical manner. They should not try to seek false reputations through meaningless accomplishments, and they should firmly oppose the tendencies of formalism, bureaucracy, hedonism and extravagance, which officials and the public vehemently oppose. Through their own example, they should lead the people in carrying out all work.

—Excerpts from a speech at the discussion session with national model workers, April 28, 2013

Today, we are closer than at any time in history to attaining the goal of the great rejuvenation of the Chinese nation, and we have greater confidence in achieving this goal and greater capability to do so than ever before. The last ten percent of a journey requires the biggest effort. The closer we are to achieving the goal of the great rejuvenation of the Chinese nation, the more we should redouble our efforts and not slacken our pace, and the more we must mobilize all young people to this end.

...

Currently we are facing important opportunities for development, but we are also facing unprecedented difficulties and challenges. The dream stretches out before us and the road lies at our feet. Those who master themselves are powerful, and those who strengthen themselves win. If we are to achieve our development goals, young people must work long and hard without letup.

...

My young friends, we are all young only once. Now is a time for you to make the most of your youth; and the future is a time for you to look back on it. The path of life is sometimes level, and at other times it is steep; it is sometimes smooth, and at other times it is rough; and it is sometimes straight, and at other times it is crooked. Young people are faced with a wide range of choices. But what is important is that you are guided by a correct worldview, outlook on life and sense of values when you are making the choices. The life experiences of countless successful people show that young people's choice to endure hardships is one that leads to rewards, and their choice to make a contribution is one that wins esteem. Youth is a time when people often experience some tempering, setbacks and tests that are beneficial for putting one on the right track. You need to have strength of character to experience both good and bad fortune, have a firm will to keep pressing forward in spite of repeated setbacks, remain optimistic in all circumstances, turn your failures into a driving force and learn from your experiences so that your life is raised to a higher plane. In short, the only way you can have full, warm and lasting memories of your youth with no regrets is if you work enthusiastically and energetically, tenaciously overcome all obstacles and make a contribution to the people in your youth.

—Excerpts from a speech to outstanding young people from all walks of life, May 4, 2013

China is still the largest developing country in the world. It is by no means an easy job to ensure the 1.3 billion Chinese people a happy life. China is faced with numerous difficulties and challenges on its development path. It calls for long-term, arduous efforts to realize the Chinese Dream of the great rejuvenation of the Chinese nation.

—Excerpt from the speech "Seek Common Development to Create a Better Future," at the Senate of Mexico, June 5, 2013

We need to maintain a spirit of reform and innovation in carrying out Party building. We need to better pass the tests of governance, reform and opening up, the market economy and the external environment; and we need to better overcome the dangers of laziness, inability, estrangement from the people and corruption. By doing so, our Party can better fulfill its responsibility to unite with and lead the people of all our country's ethnic groups in finishing building a moderately prosperous society in all respects and achieving the great rejuvenation of the Chinese nation.

—Excerpt from a speech at the Seventh Group Study Session of the Political Bureau of the Eighteenth CPC Central Committee, June 25, 2013

Over the past 60-plus years we have made tremendous progress and the Chinese people have stood up and become prosperous, but we still face severe and complex challenges and problems, and the tests the Party faces are far from over. These tests now manifest themselves in the Party's leadership of the people in achieving the goal of finishing building a moderately prosperous society in all respects and in adhering to and developing socialism with Chinese characteristics. All leading officials and Party members need to keep up their good work in the "tests" the people give the Party and in the "tests" the Party is now experiencing and will be subject to in the future. Since the Party's Eighteenth National Congress, the new central leadership has taken up the great responsibility the Party, the country and the people have passed to it, and we must not let them down.

—Excerpt from a speech made when investigating and guiding the educational and practical activities concerning the Party's mass line in Hebei, July 11– 12, 2013

We have the confidence, conditions and ability to achieve our goals. At the same time, we are soberly aware that China remains the largest developing country in the world and we will still face many difficulties and challenges on the road ahead. To enable all the Chinese people to lead a better life, we must work hard and untiringly for a long time to come. We will unwaveringly adhere to reform and opening up, steadfastly take the path of socialism with Chinese characteristics, concentrate on managing our own affairs well, continue to promote modernization, and constantly raise the people's living standards.

—Excerpt from the speech "Hand in Hand Building a China-ASEAN Community of Shared Destiny," to the Indonesian Parliament, October 3, 2013

Dreams start with study and undertakings start with practice. In today's world, knowledge and information are quickly updated, and anyone who slacks even a little in their studies will fall behind. Some people say that everyone's world is a circle, and that knowledge is its radius. The bigger the radius, the vaster the world.

...

In China, if you want to accomplish something and make a contribution, the key to success is to set off from the motherland, embrace the expectations of its people, identify the point of convergence between your skills and the country's social development and between advanced knowledge and the country's national conditions, and genuinely get your creativity to take root and bear fruit.

—Excerpts from a speech at the centenary celebration event of the Western Returned Scholars Association, October 21, 2013

To realize the Chinese Dream, we must ultimately rely on the hard work of all the people. Good fortune will not happen suddenly on its own. We especially need to strengthen the education of our young people so that they can embrace the idea of doing hard, honest and creative work from an early age. We cannot allow them to develop the wrong attitude of being a lazy glutton, leading a life of leisure, idling away one's time, advancing through life by dubious means and enjoying the fruits of someone else's labor. This is a long-term plan that has a direct bearing on the development of our nation, and we must implement it well. We should foster the fine qualities of our country's working class throughout society and energetically publicize the exemplary deeds of model workers and other role models. We should get the view that labor is what is most honorable, most sublime, most excellent and most beautiful to become the prevailing trend; and get all the people to have greater enthusiasm for labor and release their creative potential to create a better life through labor.

—Excerpt from a group discussion with the new leading body of the All-China Federation of Trade Unions, October 23, 2013

图书在版编目(CIP)数据

中华民族伟大复兴的中国梦: 英文/习近平著; 中共中央文献研究室编; 中共中央马克思恩格斯列宁斯大林著作编译局译.— 北京: 外文出版社, 2014

ISBN 978-7-119-08696-5

I. ①中… II. ①习…②中…③中… III. ①习近平－讲话－学习参考资料－英文②社会主义建设模式－中国－学习参考资料－英文IV. ①D2-0 ②D616

中国版本图书馆CIP数据核字(2014)第029389号

中华民族伟大复兴的中国梦
习近平

©外文出版社有限责任公司

外文出版社有限责任公司出版发行

(中国北京百万庄大街24号)

邮政编码 100037

http://www.flp.com.cn

北京蓝空印刷厂印刷

2014年（16开）第1版

2014年第1版第1次印刷

（英）

ISBN 978-7-119-08696-5

08000